War Horse

LEVEL TWO   700 HEADWORDS

Great Clarendon Street, Oxford, OX2 6DP, United Kingdom

Oxford University Press is a department of the University of Oxford.
It furthers the University's objective of excellence in research, scholarship,
and education by publishing worldwide. Oxford is a registered trade
mark of Oxford University Press in the UK and in certain other countries

This simplified edition © Oxford University Press 2013

The moral rights of the author have been asserted

First published in Dominoes 2013

2021

10 9 8

Original English language edition first published in 1982 under the title *War Horse* by
Egmont UK Limited, 239 Kensington High Street, London W8 6SA

Copyright © 1982 Michael Morpurgo

ISBN: 978 0 19 424982 9   Book
ISBN: 978 0 19 424966 9   Book and MultiROM Pack
MultiROM not available separately

Printed in China

This book is printed on paper from certified and well-managed sources

ACKNOWLEDGEMENTS

Cover images: Corbis (Horses/DLILLC), (Verdun battlefield 1966/Manuel Litran).
Illustrations by: Martin Impey
The publisher would like to thank the following for kind permission to reproduce photographs:
Bridgeman Art Library Ltd pp.58 (Over the Top, 1st Artists' Rifles at Marcoing, 30th
December 1917, 1918, Nash, John Northcote (1893–1977)/Imperial War Museum,
London, UK), 59 (Charge of Flowerdew's Squadron, c.1918, Munnings, Sir Alfred (1878–
1959)/© Canadian War Museum, Ottawa, Canada), 60 ((2242) The Menin Road, 1919,
Nash, Paul (1889–1946)/Imperial War Museum, London, UK), 60 (After the Recapture
of Bapaume, 1918, Nevinson, Christopher Richard Wynne (1889–1946)/© Rochdale Art
Gallery, Lancashire, UK).

DOMINOES

Series Editors: Bill Bowler and Sue Parminter

War Horse

Michael Morpurgo

Text adaptation by Alex Raynham

Illustrated by Martin Impey

Michael Morpurgo is an English author and storyteller. He is most famous for his children's stories, and was the third British Children's Laureate, from 2003–2005. He has received many awards for his writing. In 1976, Michael and his wife, Clare, started the charity *Farms for City Children*. It enables city primary school children to try living and working in the countryside for a week. Michael's book *War Horse* has been broadcast on radio and adapted as a stage play featuring life-sized horse puppets. It was made into a film, directed by Steven Spielberg, in 2011.

OXFORD
UNIVERSITY PRESS

BEFORE READING

1 *War Horse* **is about a horse called Joey. What do you think he does in the story? Tick three sentences.**

a He works in the country in England. ☐

b He goes by ship to Africa. ☐

c He pulls a big gun. ☐

d He carries an important letter. ☐

e He helps soldiers who are hurt. ☐

f He dies in France in the end. ☐

2 **Here are some other characters from** *War Horse*. **Match them with the sentences below. Use a dictionary to help you.**

1 Albert **2** Albert's father **3** Captain Nicholls

4 Topthorn **5** Emilie **6** Friedrich

a .... is very ill, but she looks after Joey and Topthorn. ☐

b .... is a British officer. He draws pictures of Joey. ☐

c .... goes to war because he wants to find his horse. ☐

d .... is a kind German soldier. He hates the war. ☐

e .... has a farm and sells Joey. ☐

f .... pulls a gun with Joey and is a good friend. ☐

3 **Which characters from Activity 2 do you think meet in the story? Compare answers with a partner.**

CHAPTER 1
Joey

Joey
By Captain James Nicholls, autumn 1914

On the wall of an old school building in Devon, England, there is a **painting** of a horse. It is a beautiful, strong animal with four white '**socks**' on its legs, and a white star on its head.

Today, the villagers meet in this building, and use it for dinners and parties. Everyone in the village knows the painting under the old clock, but few of them have stopped to read the words below it.

> ## Joey
> ### By **Captain** James Nicholls, autumn 1914

These days, few people in the village can remember the real Joey. This story is about him, the people who knew him, and the **war** in which they lived and died.

painting a coloured picture

sock a white mark at the bottom of a horse's leg

captain the leader of a group of soldiers

war fighting between countries

I will always remember the animal market. I was just six months old. I stood with my mother in a noisy ring of people who shouted all around me. They sold my mother quickly and took her away. I tried to follow her, but I couldn't. I ran around in circles. It took longer for them to sell me, but in the end, they took me out of the ring too.

'I didn't pay much for him,' a man with a red face said to his friends. Three or four men came towards me. They were laughing, and I moved away from them. Then, far away, I heard my mother's voice. I tried to jump over a wall and escape to her, but it was too high. Suddenly, the men caught me. They pushed me to the ground and sat on me. Then they put a **halter** over my head.

'You're a real fighter, aren't you?' my new buyer said. 'But I'll break you. You'll do anything that I want after that.'

They **tied** me to the back of a horse and **cart**. After that, we left the market, and I never saw my mother again.

My neck hurt while an old horse pulled the cart – and me – along the country roads. I was tired, afraid, and wet with **sweat** when we arrived at a **farm**. The halter hurt my head, too. The man put the old horse into the **stable** next to me. While she was going inside, she stopped and looked at me. She had kind eyes, and she **neighed** softly. I felt better then because I knew that I wasn't alone.

'Get in there, Zoey!' the man shouted, hitting her. Then he went away. Later, I heard voices from the farm house. A young boy and his mother came into the stables.

'Look at him, Mother. Isn't he beautiful?' the boy said. He opened the stable door.

'Father says that you mustn't touch him tonight, Albert,' his mother told him.

halter you put these ropes round the head of a horse when you want to tie it to something

tie to keep something in place with rope

cart a wooden car that a horse pulls

sweat water that comes from your body when you are hot or worried

farm a place in the country where people keep cows, sheep, and other animals

stable a building for horses to sleep in at night or live in during the winter

neigh to make a noise (of a horse)

'But he's hot and tired,' Albert answered. 'I have to **look after** him.' He turned to his mother. 'Have you ever seen a horse with a white star like that?' he asked. Then he smiled and said, 'I shall ride him everywhere.'

'You're just thirteen, Albert,' his mother replied. 'You're too young to ride him, and he's too young for it.'

Albert took off his jacket and used it to take the sweat off me. Then he brought me cold water, and sweet **hay** to eat. I neighed, and he touched my nose.

'We'll be friends, you and I,' Albert said. 'I'll call you Joey. I'll always look after you, I **promise**.'

'You shouldn't talk to horses,' Albert's mother told him when they left the stables. 'They're stupid animals, your father says.'

'He doesn't understand them,' answered Albert. I stood and watched Albert while he and his mother walked back to the house. I knew then that I had a friend for life.

look after to do things for someone or something that needs help

hay dry grass; horses eat this

promise to say that you will certainly do something

Albert and I spent a lot of time together over the next few years. When he wasn't at school or helping his father on the farm, he was with me. He often took me across the fields to a place by the Torridge River. There, he slowly began to teach me things. At first, we just walked around in circles, but later I learnt to **trot**. On the way back to the stables, Albert walked in front and **whistled** to me. I didn't have to follow his whistle, but I wanted to. He whistled like a bird, and I never forgot the sound.

There were cows, sheep, and other animals, and fields of hay on the farm. So life there was busy. Early every morning, Albert's father came and took Zoey out of the stables. They worked together all day in the fields. They broke the ground and cut the hay, and Zoey pulled the hay cart. I spent every summer in the fields, too. I didn't work like Zoey, but I watched her, and she often neighed to me. When the cold winter months came, I stayed in the stables. Albert sometimes visited me. But when he didn't, I was alone. I didn't like that.

Albert's father wasn't a bad man really. Sometimes, he was even nice to me and Zoey. But I never forgot what he did to me that first day at the market. When he came into a field, I always tried to stay away from him. Every Tuesday night, Albert's father went into the village to meet his friends. He usually came back late, and was loud and angry then. When he was like that, Zoey and I were afraid of him. Albert had to go into the village on Tuesdays too, because he rang the church **bells** with some of the other villagers. Before he went, he always put me and Zoey into the same stable.

'Don't worry. You'll be OK,' Albert told us. 'He won't come into the stable when you're together.'

One autumn evening, Zoey and I stood in the stables and listened to the church bells. When night came, we were soon

trot to run with short, quick steps (of a horse)

whistle to make a musical noise with your mouth; a musical noise that comes from your mouth

bell a metal thing that makes a noise when you move it

4

asleep. Suddenly, a light woke us up. There was someone in the stables. At first I thought that it was Albert, but then I heard his father's deep voice. When he opened the stable door, I saw that he was holding a **whip**.

'You think that you're special, don't you, Joey?' he said angrily. 'But you aren't special, my boy. Not any more. Farmer Easton says that you'll never be a good farm horse. But I'll show him. You're going to work on the farm. And if you give me any trouble, I'll hit you – see!'

Zoey neighed and moved to the back of the stable. The farmer lifted the whip. When he moved behind me, I **kicked** him as hard as I could. He cried and fell to the ground.

'You'll be sorry for that! Very sorry!' he shouted, leaving the stable angrily.

whip a special long, thin stick that people use to hit animals

kick to hit something with your feet

ACTIVITIES

READING CHECK

Correct the mistakes in these false sentences.

brown

a Joey is a ~~black~~ horse with a white star on his head.

b You can see a painting of Joey in an old stable building in Devon.

c Joey sees his father for the last time at a horse market.

d Albert loves Joey, but he is too young to buy him.

e Joey soon learns to walk in circles and to jump.

f When Albert sings, Joey follows him.

g It is a busy farm, and Joey works in the fields every day.

h On Tuesday nights, Albert's brother goes into the village to meet his friends.

i Zoey kicks Albert's father when he comes into the stables with a whip.

WORD WORK

1 Use the picture clues to complete the sentences with words from Chapter 1.

a This is Captain Nicholls's . . painting . . of Joey.

b Zoey pulls the . . . . on the farm.

c At night, they put the horses into the
. . . .

d You put a . . . . over a horse's head.

e Albert gives the horses water and lots of
. . . .

f Albert's father often carries a . . . .

2 **Find six new words or phrases from Chapter 1 around Joey. There are more letters than you need. Use the words in the correct form to complete the sentences.**

a A lot of soldiers died in the First World . . . . . . War. . . . . . .

b A . . . . is an important soldier in the army.

c At the horse market, some men . . . . Joey to a cart.

d Albert . . . . the horses. He takes food and water to them.

e Joey has got a white star on his head and four white . . . . on his legs.

f Joey and Zoey can't talk, but they . . . . a lot.

GUESS WHAT

What happens in the next chapter? Read each sentence and write *Yes* or *No*.

a Albert begins to ride Joey. . . . .

b Albert's father sells Zoey. . . . .

c Albert doesn't agree with his father. . . . .

d The War begins. . . . .

e Albert goes to France as a soldier. . . . .

CHAPTER 2
A farm horse

Early the next morning, Albert and his father came into the stables. Albert's father was **limping** badly, and Albert's eyes were red from crying.

'I wanted to shoot that horse last night,' Albert's father said, 'but your mother stopped me. Farmer Easton and I have got a **bet**. He says that Joey won't ever be a good farm horse, but I say that in a week's time he can be. I'm giving you seven days to **train** him. But if I lose that bet, I'll sell him.'

'I'll train him,' Albert replied. 'But you must promise me one thing. Never hit him again. You can't teach him anything that way. I know him, Father.'

'It doesn't matter to me how you do it, Albert,' his father replied. 'And I won't go near Joey again. But remember my words.'

After he left, Albert looked into my eyes. He was very angry.

'Are you stupid, Joey?' he said. 'Never kick anyone again! He nearly killed you last night.'

Then he spoke more softly. 'Zoey and I are going to train you,' he said, 'and it'll be hard work. You haven't got the body of a farm horse, but you have to learn to **plough**. My father will sell you – or shoot you – if he doesn't win that bet!'

That morning, Albert took me and Zoey out into the fields, and I began to pull a plough. My neck hurt, and it was hard to pull in a straight **line**. But Zoey showed me what to do. Albert shouted from behind. He didn't speak to me softly all that week. When I wasn't trying hard, he used the whip on me!

At the end of each day, I was tired and my body hurt. But after a night's rest, I was ready to work again. Slowly, I learnt how to

limp to walk unevenly because you have a bad leg

bet to agree to win money if you are right about something and to lose money if you are wrong

train to teach someone to do something well

plough to cut the ground in a field; a large tool that farmers use to do this

line a long thin mark; people standing one behind the other, or next to each other

plough, and Albert didn't use his whip so often. At the end of one long afternoon, Albert put his arms around my neck.

'You've done it!' he said. 'You're a farm horse now, Joey. Farmer Easton and father were watching you today. You did well, so father won his bet.' Albert **patted** Zoey's and my noses. 'You dear things, I could **kiss** you both,' he said, 'but I won't, because I know that they're watching!'

All that summer, I worked on the farm with Zoey. We ploughed the fields and pulled the cart, and Albert whistled and talked to us. One evening on the way back to the stables, Albert stopped whistling and told us, 'Mother says that there's going to be a war with Germany soon.' He patted my head. 'But we'll be OK,' he said. 'I'm just fifteen. I'm too young to be a soldier.'

Then he laughed. 'Perhaps you'll work as a war horse one day, Joey. And perhaps I'll be a soldier one day too!'

pat to touch an animal lovingly with your hand

kiss to touch lovingly with your mouth

9

A few weeks later, we were in the stables one evening when I heard Albert's father in the **yard**.

'The war's started,' he shouted. 'We'll show those Germans now!' Zoey and I looked over our stable doors. Albert's mother was standing outside the house.

'Dear **God**, help us!' she said quietly, her hand over her mouth.

That summer, Albert began to ride me. He started slowly at first, but soon I knew all the roads and fields around the village. After work, he rode me down to the river and we **galloped** up the hill on the other side. Albert was a good rider. He didn't pull on the **reins**, but used his knees and feet to show me what he wanted from me.

The war was far away from us at first, but Albert's **parents** often talked about the future. Everyone was worried, and Albert and his father often argued.

'I work hard on the farm, but nothing ever pleases him,' Albert told his mother in the yard.

'You mustn't be angry with him,' his mother said. 'When we bought this farm, we did it for you. But we borrowed a lot of money. This war will bring hard times for farmers. How are we going to pay the bank? He's a good man, Albert, so try to understand him.' But Albert and his father didn't speak much all summer.

One day, Albert's father told him to take an animal to the next village. Albert didn't want to go, but in the end he agreed. After he left, Albert's father took me out of the stables. I was surprised, but Zoey was with us, so I didn't feel worried. We pulled the cart to the village.

yard an empty place near a house; like a garden but with no trees or flowers

God an important being who never dies and who decides what happens in the world

gallop to move fast (of a horse)

reins strings that are tied to a horse's head and that you pull to make it go one way or the other

parent a mother or father

When we arrived, I heard music and saw crowds of people. Young men from the village were waiting in lines. They wanted to fight in the war. A young captain with dark hair came towards us. He patted me and looked at my teeth.

'Last night, you told me that he was a good horse,' he said to Albert's father, 'and you were right. I'd like to ride him myself.'

'So will you pay me forty pounds, then, Captain Nicholls? That's what we agreed,' Albert's father said.

'Yes, if the **vet** thinks that he's OK,' the captain replied. So they took me to the vet, and then the captain paid the money.

'You'll be fine, Joey,' Albert's father said to me. 'They'll look after you.' There were **tears** in his eyes. 'I know that you don't understand,' he said. 'And Albert loves you – so he won't understand. But the farm needs money.'

Zoey neighed and fought, but Albert's father drove the cart away. I began to neigh. Just then, Albert ran through the crowd and put his arms around my neck.

'This is my horse!' he cried.

vet a doctor for animals

tear the water that comes from your eyes when you cry

ACTIVITIES

READING CHECK

Match the sentences with the people who say them.

a I wanted to shoot that horse last night. ☐ 4

b Are you stupid, Joey? ☐

c The war's started. ☐

d Nothing ever pleases him. ☐

e When we bought this farm, we did it for you. ☐

f You told me that he was a good horse. ☐

g They'll look after you. ☐

h This is my horse! ☐

1 ☐ Albert's mother says this to Albert.
2 ☐ Albert's father says this to Joey.
3 ☐ Albert says this to his mother.
4 ☑ Albert's father says this to Albert.
5 ☐ Albert says this to Captain Nicholls.
6 ☐ Albert says this to Joey.
7 ☐ Captain Nicholls says this to Albert's father.
8 ☐ Albert's father says this to his wife.

WORD WORK

1 Find nine more new words from Chapter 2 in the wordsquare.

p	z	c	t	o	j	x	n	p	a
t	e	a	r	s	k	f	l	a	r
w	k	y	a	r	d	j	e	r	g
t	m	k	i	s	s	i	v	e	t
v	i	g	n	q	n	a	r	n	p
g	a	l	l	o	p	s	d	t	o
j	s	z	i	r	e	i	n	s	f
n	p	m	n	e	n	u	j	s	i
z	g	b	e	t	j	e	f	c	b

12

2 Use the words from Activity 1 to complete the sentences.

a Albert's father doesn't want to lose his ...... *bet* ...... with Farmer Easton.

b Albert has to .... Joey to be a farm horse in one week.

c It is difficult for Joey to plough in a straight ....

d 'I could .... you both,' Albert tells the horses.

e Albert is a good rider. He doesn't pull on the ....

f They go down to river and Joey .... up the hill.

g Albert often doesn't agree with his ....

h Albert's father is shouting in the .... , so his mother comes out of the house.

i The .... checks Joey before Captain Nicholls buys him.

j When Albert's father leaves Joey, there are .... in his eyes.

GUESS WHAT

What happens in the next chapter? Tick two boxes each for a, b and c.

a Albert...
   1 wants to be a soldier. ☐
   2 goes to France. ☐
   3 promises to find Joey. ☐

b Joey...
   1 meets a new friend. ☐
   2 learns to be an army horse. ☐
   3 kicks a soldier. ☐

c Captain Nicholls...
   1 gives Joey back to Albert. ☐
   2 makes a picture of Joey. ☐
   3 talks to Joey about the war. ☐

CHAPTER 3
Going to France

Albert looked at Captain Nicholls. 'My father sold Joey to you, didn't he?' he said. 'Well, if you take my horse to war, I'll go with him.'

Captain Nicholls answered kindly. 'You're ready to fight, but you're too young and you know it. Come back when you're seventeen.'

'So I can't do anything now,' Albert said.

'No,' the captain replied. 'But what's your name, young man?'

'Narracott, **sir** – Albert Narracott.'

'Well, Mr Narracott, this could be a long war. We'll need people like you in the **cavalry**. When you're older, tell them my name – Captain Nicholls. And don't worry about Joey. I'll look after him for you, I promise.'

Albert tried to smile. He patted my nose and touched my ears. 'I'll find you again, Joey,' he said. 'I don't know how, but I'll find you.' Then he turned and walked sadly away.

sir you say this when you talk to an important man

cavalry soldiers who fight on horses

throw (*past* **threw**, **thrown**) to make something move quickly through the air

draw (*past* **drew**, **drawn**) to make a picture with a pen or pencil

My first few weeks in the army were very difficult. Our trainers rode us around the riding school. On other days, we waited for hours under the hot sun. My trainer, Perkins, was a short man who used his whip a lot. All the men and horses were afraid of him. I tried to **throw** him off my back a few times, but he always understood what I wanted to do, and he never fell. Over many weeks, I learnt how to be a cavalry horse.

Captain Nicholls visited me every evening. I was happy to see him because he talked to me, like Albert. He often brought pencils and paper, and he **drew** my picture.

'I'm going to make a painting of you soon,' he said one evening. 'It'll be a fine picture because you're a beautiful horse. I'm going to send it to Albert. Then he'll know that I'm looking after you.'

He looked up at me, then drew, then looked again. And he talked to me all the time.

'It's my hope that the war ends before Albert's seventeen,' he said. 'Because the fighting will be terrible. Most of the **officers** in our **unit** think that this war will be easy, but Captain Stewart and I don't agree with them.' His face darkened. 'I tell you, Joey, a few **machine guns** can stop the best cavalry in the world.'

Just then, Perkins came into the stables. 'Are you drawing him again, sir?' he asked.

'I'm trying to,' the captain answered. 'Isn't he beautiful?'

'Yes, he is,' my trainer replied. 'But being beautiful isn't everything, sir. Not in a war.'

'Be careful what you say about my horse,' the captain went on angrily. 'And look after him well.' Then he walked out of the stables.

officer a leader of a group of soldiers, for example, a captain

unit many soldiers that fight together in a group

machine gun a gun that shoots again and again very fast

charge when soldiers run at the enemy; to run at the enemy

sword a long knife for fighting

proud happy about something that someone has done

A few days later, Captain Nicholls rode me for the first time. We trained together all day. Captain Nicholls was in front of his unit, and next to him was his friend, Captain Stewart. At the end of the day, our cavalry unit was ready to **charge**. While the men held up their **swords** and shouted, I looked at Captain Stewart's beautiful black horse, Topthorn. He was stronger and taller than me, but he had kind eyes. We galloped across the field together, faster and faster. Neither of us wanted to lose, and we left the other horses behind us. Once we were at the other side of the field, we stopped. Both captains talked about their horses, and how we were the best in the cavalry. They were **proud** of us.

That night, they put Topthorn in the stable next to me, and the next day we were together on the ship to France. The weather was stormy, and many horses neighed and kicked. The soldiers came down and stayed with us, but Topthorn helped me the most. I rested my head on his body while the ship went up and down. I tried to be strong, like him.

The men were excited about going to war. But when we got off the ship in France, we saw hundreds of **wounded** soldiers. They limped past us, or people carried them onto the ship. When we looked at their faces, we were silent.

It was a long walk to the **front line**, and everyone soon forgot about the wounded soldiers. The men laughed and sang. Topthorn and I walked together, and Captain Nicholls and Captain Stewart talked. They were kind men, and they looked after us well. Often, to give us a rest, they stopped riding and walked next to us. Captain Nicholls was a big man, but he was a good rider. He didn't feel heavy on my back.

We stopped for a few minutes every hour, and the soldiers often brought us water. Topthorn always shook his head after he drank, and cold water fell on my hot face. In the end, we were near the front line, and the terrible sound of the guns was louder. At night, there were **flashes** of light in the sky, but Topthorn helped me. I didn't feel so afraid with him next to me.

The soldiers talked a lot, and we learnt what was happening from them. Some German units were trying to move behind the British army, and we had to find them. We walked around looking for the enemy for days. Then suddenly, we found them. They were in a field on the other side of a wood.

The officers shouted to the men. The soldiers took out their swords, and we walked into the wood in a line. Captain Nicholls was talking to me.

'Take it easy, Joey,' he said. 'Don't be excited. We'll be fine, don't you worry.'

I looked across at Topthorn while we moved through the trees. He was trotting now, and waiting for the sound of the **bugle**. Then suddenly, the bugle sounded and we charged out of the wood and into the light.

wounded hurt, often with a hole in the body

front line the line between two armies; soldiers fight here

flash a sudden bright light

bugle soldiers play notes on this instrument to give a signal

17

ACTIVITIES

READING CHECK

Tick the correct sentences and correct the false sentences.

a Albert is too ill to fight in the war. ☐

...Albert is too young to fight in the war....

b Captain Nicholls promises to look after Joey. ☐

....

c At the riding school, Joey learns to be a war horse. ☐

....

d All the horses and men are proud of Joey's trainer. ☐

....

e Captain Nicholls photographs Joey. ☐

....

f Captain Nicholls doesn't think that the war will be easy. ☐

....

g Joey and Topthorn are the slowest horses in their unit. ☐

....

h They see dead soldiers when they arrive in France. ☐

....

i It takes the unit days to find the enemy. ☐

....

WORD WORK

1 Unscramble the words to match the pictures.

a erciffo ...officer... **b** glube .... **c** wrad ....

d sdorw .... **e** rgchae .... **f** torwh ....

18

2 Use the words in the box to complete Captain Nicholls's diary.

officers   wounded
machine   unit
cavalry   proud
front   ~~flashes~~

October 22nd, 1914

I am writing this at night. There are **a)** ....flashes.... of light in the sky, because we are near the **b)** .... line now. We arrived in France yesterday. When we got off the ship, we saw long lines of **c)** .... soldiers. It was terrible to see them, but the men soon forgot about them. They are excited about going to war!

The other **d)** .... in my **e)** .... think that this war is going to be easy, but Captain Stewart and I don't agree. We have fine horses, and we are **f)** .... of them. But how can men on horses fight against **g)** .... guns? A few of those guns in the right place can stop the best **h)** .... in the world.

We will meet the enemy soon, and I will try to do my best when we do. Perhaps I will live to see my home again.

GUESS WHAT

Tick three things that you think will happen in the next chapter.

a Captain Nicholls dies. ☐

b Joey is very ill. ☐

c Someone new rides Joey. ☐

d Joey and Topthorn find Germans around them. ☐

e A German soldier shoots Topthorn dead. ☐

f The unit goes back to England. ☐

CHAPTER 4
The cavalry charge

The men shouted as we charged down the hill. In the field below us, German soldiers in grey **uniforms** stopped and turned. And then we heard their guns.

Suddenly, I had no rider. I was soon in front of everyone. I couldn't stop or turn with all those horses behind me, so I galloped on towards the enemy. The Germans moved out of the way as I crashed through their lines.

uniform a suit of clothes that is the same for everyone; soldiers wear it

I wanted to run on and on, away from the guns. But Captain Stewart found me and took me back to the unit.

'We won,' the British soldiers said, and they told stories about the **battle**. But there were dead and wounded horses and men everywhere. We lost a quarter of the unit that day.

'He was proud of you, Joey. I'm sure of that,' Captain Stewart told me. 'He died in that charge today, and you finished it for him.'

That night, I thought about poor Captain Nicholls. Topthorn stood over me for hours, before I went to sleep.

Early the next morning, Captain Stewart came to see us. There was a **trooper** with him. He was very young and he had a red face. When I looked at him, I thought of Albert.

'This is Joey,' Captain Stewart told the trooper. 'He was my best friend's horse, so look after him.' Then he stood near me and said quietly in my ear, 'and you look after Trooper Warren, Joey. He's just a boy, and his horse died yesterday.'

Trooper Warren wasn't a good rider. He felt heavy on my back and he pulled on the reins a lot, but he was very kind to me. I couldn't ride with Topthorn any more because the troopers rode behind the officers. But when we stopped, Trooper Warren always took me to see Topthorn.

Day after day, we looked for enemy units. When we found them, the troopers went off to fight. They usually got off their horses just before they fought, and after every battle there were a few horses without riders. During those long days and nights, Trooper Warren began to talk to me. He told me about his family, how he didn't want to fight, and how his horse died in battle.

'I tell you, Joey,' he said, 'I didn't want to get on another horse after that battle. But you've helped me. I'm not afraid any more.'

battle when two armies fight

trooper an ordinary cavalry soldier, not an officer

21

Winter soon came, and it rained all the time. On both sides of the front line, the armies made deep, long **trenches**. The ground was too soft for cavalry horses, so they took us back behind the front line. The soldiers and horses were wet all the time. At night, we stood in deep, cold **mud**. After months of rain and snow, many horses went to the **veterinary** hospital. Most of them didn't come back. Even big, strong Topthorn had a bad **cough**, but we lived through that terrible winter because Trooper Warren and Captain Stewart looked after us well. When they came down the lines of horses at night, Topthorn and I were very happy to see them. Trooper Warren sometimes had letters from his mother in England. When nobody was around, he read them to me.

'Sally from the village says that she'll write soon,' he read aloud one day. Then he looked up at me. 'That's my girl, Joey,' he explained. 'After the war, I'm going to marry her.'

One spring night, the guns didn't stop. Early the next morning, the troopers came down the lines of horses. We were going into battle again. They rode us along the country roads. When the sun came up, they were singing songs. We went through an empty village, then **reached** the front line. Thousands of soldiers were waiting in the trenches. While we rode past them, they called out to us. There was no green here: only mud, holes, and black trees. In front of us, we could see a hill with a wood, and long lines of **barbed wire**. The troopers took out their swords, and we trotted. Then we heard the sound of the bugle.

'Do your best, Joey,' Trooper Warren cried when we started to gallop. 'I want to be proud of you.'

trench a long, narrow hole in the ground to hide in when fighting

mud very wet, soft ground

veterinary for looking after animals

cough when you make a noise in your throat because you are ill; to make a noise in your throat

reach to arrive at a place

barbed wire long circles of very thin metal with sharp knives on them

22

At first, it was quiet. Then I heard the sound of the guns and the terrible cries of wounded horses and men. The ground shook, and more and more of us fell while we galloped up the hill towards the wood.

'Oh God! The barbed wire's still in one piece!' Trooper Warren shouted on my back. Very few of us reached that barbed wire, and fewer found a way through it. We jumped over the first German trenches, but they were empty. The shots were coming from the wood.

There weren't many of us now, but we rode on towards the wood. Then we saw more barbed wire between the trees. It was too late for some horses. They caught their legs in the barbed wire and died there with their riders. I saw Topthorn in front of me. In one place, the barbed wire wasn't so high and he jumped over it. I followed him into the wood. Suddenly, we were alone. Then German soldiers came out from behind the trees. Captain Stewart and Trooper Warren stopped. There were guns all around us.

READING CHECK

Correct ten more mistakes in the chapter summary.

                                                          Germans
Joey's cavalry unit wins their first battle with the ~~British~~, but they lose one half of their men

and horses, and Captain Stewart dies. The next day, Joey meets his new rider – Trooper Warren.

Warren is not a bad rider but a very nice man. He talks to Joey and tells him about his family.

When the summer comes, the armies make long roads on either side of the front line. The

ground is too hard for cavalry horses, so they stay behind the front line. It rains all the time, and

a lot of the horses are ill, but Trooper Warren looks after Joey. When nobody is around, he reads

Joey books from his mother in England.

In the winter, Joey's unit goes back to war. They charge towards the enemy, and most

of them die. Suddenly, Joey and Topthorn are alone with their riders in a trench. Then they see

enemy horses all around them.

WORD WORK

Read the clues and complete the puzzle with new words from chapter 4 in the correct form. Write the mystery word in the grey boxes.

1 It takes Joey's unit a long time to .... *reach* .... the front line.
2 In the winter, both armies make long .... in the ground.
3 Captain Nicholls dies in his first ....
4 Horses can't jump over .... wire.
5 Topthorn is very ill during the winter. He has a bad ....
6 Joey's new rider is a young cavalry ....

Mystery word: ....

GUESS WHAT

What happens in the next chapter? Choose an ending to complete each sentence.

a Captain Stewart and Trooper Warren …
  1 die in battle. ☐
  2 are suddenly prisoners. ☐

b Joey and Topthorn …
  1 work as German cavalry horses. ☐
  2 pull a cart. ☐

c The German soldiers …
  1 leave Joey and Topthorn in the wood. ☐
  2 take Joey and Topthorn to a hospital. ☐

d A French girl and her grandfather …
  1 look after Joey and Topthorn. ☐
  2 buy the horses from the Germans. ☐

CHAPTER 5
The ambulance cart

The German soldiers watched us, but they didn't shoot. 'Drop your sword, trooper,' Captain Stewart said. 'Too many people have died already today.'

The Captain and Trooper Warren got off our backs and stood next to us, holding our reins.

'I told you that we had the best horses in the cavalry,' Captain Stewart told Trooper Warren. 'And I was right.'

Then the Germans took us out of the wood. Behind us, dead horses and men were lying on the barbed wire.

'Look at all of them,' said the Captain, angrily.

'What will happen to the horses?' Trooper Warren asked.

'They're prisoners like us,' Captain Stewart replied. 'But don't worry. The Germans love horses like the British.'

They patted us, and then the Germans took them away. While they walked down the road, Captain Stewart put his arm around Trooper Warren. Then soldiers took Topthorn and me down the hill to an army hospital.

When we arrived, there were wounded German soldiers all

around us. They patted our heads and talked to us. A tall, wounded officer limped towards us.

'Find food and water for these horses,' he said. 'They came through fire today. We should look after them.'

Just then, a doctor came and spoke to the officer. 'There are hundreds of German and British wounded out there, and we haven't got many ambulances,' he said. 'We need these horses.'

'These aren't work horses. They're fine British cavalry horses,' replied the officer at first, angrily. But later he agreed, saying, 'If they go back to the front line, I'll go too, to look after them.'

So they tied us to an old farm cart, and the wounded officer and two **orderlies** took us back to the front line. We walked past long lines of tired and wounded soldiers. They had the same young, grey faces as the British. Just the uniforms were different. All afternoon and all evening we brought wounded men from the battle to the army hospital, and the guns never stopped. It was night when we came back for the last time.

'These horses **saved** a lot of lives today,' the wounded officer told the doctor. 'Good German lives and good British lives. So look after them.' He waved at us while they took him away to hospital. The orderlies took us to a farm and put us in a warm stable with lots of hay and water. Topthorn and I were very tired, and we soon went to sleep.

Some time later, lights woke us. Topthorn and I stood up and moved to the back of the stable. We were afraid, but then we heard French voices. It was an old farmer and his granddaughter.

'These horses are beautiful, grandfather,' the granddaughter said. 'Can I have them?' Her name was Emilie. She was thin and she had a white face.

orderly a soldier who helps in an army hospital

save to take someone or something out of danger

Every day, we pulled our ambulance cart along the dangerous roads to the front line. Sometimes **shells** hit the fields around us. We saved a lot of men that summer, and the soldiers loved us for that. One day, a young German soldier with a wounded arm put his good arm around my neck and kissed me.

'Thank you, my friend,' he said. 'I didn't think that I could get out of there, but you rescued me.' He put a **medal** around my neck.

'I found this in the mud yesterday,' he explained. 'At first I thought that I would **keep** it, but now I think that you should have it – both of you. They say that you're English horses,' he laughed. 'But now you've got a German medal.'

They put the medal outside our stable door, and men from the hospital often visited us. Topthorn and I were always happy to see them. They patted us and talked to us, and sometimes they brought sweet apples for us. The orderlies at the hospital didn't know anything about horses, so Emilie and her grandfather looked after us when we came back from the front line. They gave us water and hay. They **brushed** us and put more hay on the floor for our beds. On summer evenings, Emilie took us out into the fields and stayed with us. She took us back to the stables when her grandfather called.

'You're both very **brave**,' she told us. 'And I'm proud of you.'

When the winter came, we stayed in the stables. Emilie climbed up to the floor above us and threw down our hay. Then she lay and looked down at us. She talked to us while her grandfather was working below.

'After the war, I'll be older and stronger,' she said. 'I'm going to ride you through the woods. I'll always look after you if you stay here with me.'

shell a large metal thing that you shoot from a big gun

medal when you are brave, people give you this to wear

keep (*past* **kept**) to have with you

brush to move something through the hair on an animal's body and make it look good

brave not afraid

Every morning, Emilie watched us while we walked away from the farm. In the noise of the battle, we thought of seeing her again at night, and so we felt stronger. But one winter evening, Emilie wasn't waiting for us when we got back to the farm. Topthorn and I knew that something was wrong. It was late and snow was falling when Emilie's grandfather came into the stables. He brought us hot **oats**. Then he sat with us.

'Emilie's very ill,' he told us. 'She's just thirteen years old, but her parents and her brother have already died in this war. Now *she's* fighting for her life up there in her room. The German doctor has tried everything. Now we have to wait.'

There were tears in his eyes. 'She thinks of you every day, you know,' he said. 'So if you understand what I'm saying, please think of her tonight.'

oats these grow in fields, and horses or people can eat them

READING CHECK

Put these events from Chapter 5 in the correct order.

a ☐ The old man is very unhappy because Emilie is very ill.

b ☐ A young German soldier puts a medal around Joey's neck.

c ☐ A German doctor needs the horses to pull an ambulance cart.

d ☐ Captain Stewart tells Trooper Warren to drop his sword.

e ☐ An old French man and his granddaughter Emilie visit their stable at night.

f ☐ The Germans take Joey and Topthorn to a German army hospital.

g ☐ The summer comes, and Emilie takes the horses out into the fields.

h ☐ Joey and Topthorn go back to the front line on the German side.

i ☐ The Germans take Captain Stewart and Trooper Warren away.

WORD WORK

1 Find new words from Chapter 5 to match the pictures.

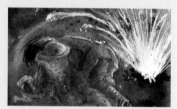

a s ⍺ v e

b o _ _ _ _ _ _ _ _

c s _ _ _ _

d m _ _ _ _

e b _ _ _ _

f o _ _ _

2 Use the words from Activity 1 in the correct form to complete the sentences.

a The ambulance cart.....*saves*.....a lot of wounded soldiers from death.

b Pulling the cart is dangerous work. Sometimes..................hit the ground near them.

c One day, a young soldier finds a..................and he gives it to Topthorn and Joey because they are so brave.

d The..................at the hospital are kind, but they don't know how to look after horses.

e Emilie and her grandfather..................the horses every night, and then they give them water to drink and hay to eat.

f When the weather is cold, the horses have hot..................to eat.

GUESS WHAT

What happens in the next chapter? Tick two pictures.

a ☐

b ☐

c ☐

d ☐

CHAPTER 6
The gun team

The guns didn't stop all night, and the orderlies took us from the stables early the next morning. Deep snow hid the holes in the road, so it took a long time for us to reach the front line. On the way back, someone remembered that it was Christmas. The wounded men sang Christmas songs and cried.

We brought back a lot of wounded soldiers that day, but in the evening, the guns stopped. Without the smoke from the shells, you could see the stars in the sky. It was a beautiful, quiet night. When we reached the farm, Emilie's grandfather was standing outside in the snow.

'It's a fine night,' he said, smiling. 'Emilie woke up, and she's feeling better. And do you know the first thing that she said? "I must take the horses their food." The German doctor didn't want her to get out of bed, so he promised to give you **extra** food all winter.'

He took us into the stables. 'Thank you,' he said. 'Because I know that you thought of her last night. Now all is well, I tell you. All is well!'

extra more than usual

And all was well for a time. When the spring came, the battles moved further away. Most days they didn't need us at the hospital, so Emilie took us out to the fields around the farm. Emilie was still very weak, and she coughed a lot, but that spring, she began to ride us. She usually rode me because Topthorn was taller and it was difficult for her to get onto him. But sometimes she climbed from my back onto Topthorn.

One afternoon, we were resting in a field when army **trucks** came into the farm yard. People called us, and we trotted across to them. They were the doctors and orderlies from the army hospital. They patted us, and then said goodbye. Emilie ran towards us.

'I've waited for this day!' she cried. 'They're taking the hospital away, but the kind German doctor says that we can keep you.'

truck a kind of big car for carrying things or people

We worked on the farm all that summer. We cut the hay, pulled carts full of apples, and ploughed the ground. At first, Emilie wasn't happy with this. She didn't want us to be work horses.

'But they like to work,' her grandfather said. 'Look at them. Are they unhappy? And we have to live.'

So Emilie looked after us, and told her grandfather not to work us too hard. We were with people who loved us, and we were happy. But nobody could be happy for long in that war.

One evening, we were in the stables when we heard a noise outside. **Teams** of horses were pulling big, heavy guns into the yard. The old soldier on the **ammunition** cart came and patted us, but the other men weren't very friendly. When they put the horses into the stables, Topthorn and I neighed at them. Most of them didn't reply because they were too tired.

Early the next morning, a thin German **major** with a dirty uniform came into the stables. He stood and looked at us, and then left. Later, he knocked on the door of the farm house.

'I'm taking your horses,' he told Emilie's grandfather. 'We need them for our guns.'

'You can't do that!' Emilie cried. 'They're *my* horses.' But her grandfather looked at her and said, 'We can't stop them, Emilie. So I want you to be brave.'

team a number of animals or people who work together

ammunition metal things that you need to shoot from guns

major an important officer in the army

Little Emilie came into the stables and put her arms around us. She was crying. 'Please come back to me,' she said quietly. 'If you don't come back, I'll die.' Then she took us out into the yard.

'I want them back later,' she told the officer, angrily. Then she turned and walked into the house. The German soldiers tied us to the ammunition cart, and the unit started to move. Emilie's grandfather watched us with tears in his eyes.

The soldiers put us into a gun team with four other horses.
Topthorn and a big, strong horse called Heinie were at the front,
and behind me there were two beautiful, golden horses. Next to
me was a thin horse called Coco. Horses and men didn't go near
Coco when he was angry, and that was most of the time!

And so we went back to the noise of battle. We pulled the gun
along the muddy roads to the front line. The soldiers worked us
hard, and they used whips – not because they were bad people,
but because they were tired and they had no time to think about
us. Only one soldier was different. The kind, old man on the
ammunition cart gave us pieces of bread, and he talked to us.
The other soldiers called him '**mad** old Friedrich' because he
spent more time with us than with them.

When the winter came, we were cold and wet all the time.
We stood all night next to the guns with mud on our bodies.
There wasn't much food, and we began to get thinner. Our legs
hurt all the time, and it was more and more difficult to pull the
heavy guns.

mad not thinking
well

Slowly, all the horses **became** ill. The soldiers tried to look after us, but the hard work and the cold weather were killing us. In a few months, big, strong Heinie became weak and ill. The vets couldn't do anything, so they took him away and shot him. A few months later, a piece of a shell killed Coco. Then one night, Topthorn started to cough again. I put my head next to him and tried to make him warm, but he didn't sleep well. The next day, the vet looked at him carefully.

'This horse needs to rest,' he told the major.

'How can he rest?' the officer replied. 'He has to pull the gun. We haven't got extra horses.'

Topthorn still had a cough when the spring came, but he was alive. The battles moved away, so we rested in the fields, ate the new spring **grass**, and became stronger. Then one day, Friedrich took us to the ammunition cart. For the next few weeks, we brought ammunition from the train station to the guns at the front line. Friedrich was good to us. He gave us extra food, and he argued when they put too many heavy shells onto the cart. Friedrich liked us both, but he loved Topthorn. He knew that Topthorn was ill, so he looked after him carefully.

'I tell you, my friends,' he said one day. 'The other men think that I'm mad. But they're mad, not me. We're killing and dying in this war, and we don't know why. Now that *is* mad.'

Suddenly his voice changed. 'I just want to be at home with my wife and children. I'd like to run away from here with you both, right now... but they shoot people who do that.'

When the autumn came, we were ready for battle again. Friedrich decided to stay with Topthorn, so he told the officer that he wanted to drive our gun team. We pulled the guns along the country roads, with Friedrich on Topthorn's back.

become (*past* **became**, **become**) to begin to be

grass it is green; gardens and fields have lots of it on the ground

One hot day, the soldiers were resting by a river. Some slept under the trees, while others took off their uniforms and swam. When we went to the river to drink, Topthorn put his head into the water and shook it, like he always did. Cold water fell onto my face. It felt wonderful. But when we were walking back through the woods, Topthorn fell suddenly to the ground. He didn't get up. I pushed his body and neighed, but he didn't move. Then I knew that he was dead.

'Why?' Friedrich shouted, angrily. 'Why does this war kill everything good?' He sat by Topthorn and cried. Soldiers stood silently around them. Just then, we heard a terrible sound. Shells began to fall around us. Suddenly, the soldiers were running up the hill and trying to escape. The ground shook and the trees burned.

'Move!' Friedrich shouted, and he tried to pull me up the hill. 'Come with me, and live,' he cried. But I couldn't leave Topthorn.

ACTIVITIES

READING CHECK

Choose the correct words to complete the sentences about Chapter 6.

a The orderlies take Joey and Topthorn to the *farm / front line* on Christmas morning.

b It is hard to get there because there is deep *mud / snow* on the road.

c When they arrive at the stables, Emilie's grandfather is very *happy / angry*.

d The hospital moves away, and Joey and Topthorn *rest / work* on the farm all summer.

e One day, a thin German officer says, 'I'm taking the horses.' He wants them to pull a *gun / cart*.

f He puts Joey and Topthorn into a team with *six / four* other horses.

g A lot of horses become ill in the cold weather. The vets *shoot / sell* them.

h A shell kills a horse called *Coco / Heinie*.

i In the spring, Friedrich uses Joey and Topthorn to pull his *hospital / ammunition* cart.

j One day, they are walking through a wood when *Friedrich / Topthorn* falls to the ground.

WORD WORK

1 Match the words from Chapter 6 with the definitions.

a extra
b major
c grass
d ammunition
e mad
f truck
g team

1 gardens and fields have a lot of this
2 people or animals who work together
3 a very important army officer
4 not thinking well
5 more than usual
6 you shoot this from guns
7 a big car for carrying things or people

2 Use the words from Activity 1 to complete the sentences.

a The medical orderlies get into a ......truck...... and drive away.

b The thin .... takes Joey and Topthorn away.

c Heinie is the strongest horse in their gun ....

d There isn't much hay in winter, but Friedrich tries to give the horses .... food.

e The unit needs a lot of .... for their guns.

f People think that Friedrich is .... because he spends more time with the horses than with other soldiers.

g In the spring, Topthorn and Joey rest in the fields and eat sweet, green ....

GUESS WHAT

What happens in the next chapter? Tick one picture for each sentence.

a Friedrich …

1 rides Joey. ☐   **2** dies. ☐

b Joey …

1 hurts his leg. ☐   **2** runs back to Emilie's farm. ☐

c Two soldiers …

1 fight to have Joey. ☐   **2** find a way to decide who has Joey. ☐

d The winner takes Joey to a …

1 veterinary hospital. ☐   **2** meat market. ☐

Chapter 7
No-man's-land

Shells hit the woods around us, but I couldn't move. The men were shouting and horses were pulling the guns up the hill, but Friedrich stayed with me.

'Come on!' he cried. Then he understood that I wanted to stay. He turned and tried to run, but it was too late. A shell hit him. He fell and died next to Topthorn. I stayed by their bodies all that day and all night. Shells fell near us, but I couldn't leave. I didn't want to be alone again.

The next morning, I was standing near my dead friends and eating grass when I heard a terrible sound. A great, grey **machine** was coming towards me. Smoke was coming out of it, and I had to run. I was too afraid. I galloped down to the river, then up the hill on the other side. When I turned and looked back, I could see more of those machines. They were crossing the river below me.

machine
something that does work for people and often moves

I didn't know which way to go, but I needed to escape. I galloped across fields, roads, and old trenches. I crossed another river, and went through empty farm yards and burning villages. That evening, the guns sounded further away. I found a field next to a river and lay on the wet grass there. Soon, I was asleep.

When I woke up, it was dark. The guns were nearer again, and there were flashes of light everywhere in the sky. I didn't know what to do, but there was food and water by the river, so I decided to stay there. Just then, I heard machine guns very near me.

I ran on into the night, and the fields started to change. There was no more grass in them – only mud, broken trees, and shell holes. I nearly fell into one big hole, and a piece of barbed wire caught my front leg. I kicked hard, and the barbed wire cut into me. I fought and tried to escape. Then suddenly my leg was free. I limped on across the muddy ground. My leg hurt badly, but I had to escape the shells. I hurried away from the flashes of light that lit the night sky. It was the longest night of my life. I felt cold and lonely, with death all around me.

Early the next morning, a **mist** came down. I couldn't see anything, but I could hear the guns and I tried to move away from them. Sometimes, when the sounds of battle were very near, I just stopped. I couldn't move because I was too afraid.

It became lighter. I still couldn't see anything through the mist, but I heard voices not far from me.

'I'm telling you, I saw something out there, **Sergeant**,' a soldier said.

'Well what was it, son?' a voice replied. 'Half the German army, or just a few of them?'

'It wasn't a man,' the soldier answered. 'It was more like a cow or a horse.'

mist a thin cloud near the ground

sergeant an important soldier, but not as important as a captain

'Out there?' the sergeant laughed. 'And how did it get into **no-man's-land**?' Then his voice changed. 'There's probably nothing out there, but we can't see anything in the mist. We don't want the Germans to come and visit us now, do we? So have your guns ready and your eyes open. That way, we'll all still be alive at breakfast time.'

The sun started to break through the mist, and slowly I began to see around me. I was standing in no-man's-land, between the two armies. On both sides, I could see lines of barbed wire and trenches. Suddenly, hundreds of people were laughing and whistling.

'Stay down, boys,' shouted a British voice, but I saw the heads of more and more British and German soldiers. They were looking out of their trenches, laughing and calling to me. I could smell hot food, and I tried to move towards the nearest trench, but the barbed wire stopped me. I turned and walked the other way. Every time, the barbed wire stopped me. I was tired and hungry. In the end, I found a little grass and started to eat.

I was still eating when a soldier in a grey uniform climbed out of the German trenches. He was waving a white **handkerchief**, and he started to cut a way through the barbed wire. Then I heard loud voices on the British side, and soon a soldier climbed out of a British trench. He came towards me, also with a white handkerchief in his hand.

The German reached me first. He had grey hair, like my poor friend Friedrich. There were pieces of black bread in his hand. When I moved towards him, he put a **rope** around me. Then I heard a shout.

'Hey! Where are you going?' the British soldier cried. He walked towards us and stopped in front of the German.

no-man's-land the place between two armies; neither side has this place

handkerchief you can cry into this; you hold up something white in war when you don't want to fight

rope a very thick, strong string

'Now what do we do?' he asked. 'I can't speak German. Can you understand me?'

'Yes, I can. I speak a little English – from school,' the older man replied. 'It is not good, but it is OK, I think. I was here first, so this is my horse.'

'I don't know about that,' the young soldier replied. But then he said, 'Just look at us. Isn't this stupid? We're fighting here, but you could be back at home in Germany and I could be back at home in Wales.'

On both sides of no-man's-land, people waited and watched while the two soldiers talked. They patted me and looked at my leg.

'We've got a veterinary hospital,' said the Welsh soldier. 'We can look after him. But perhaps you've got a hospital, too.'

coin metal money

'We have,' said the German. Then he took a **coin** out of his pocket and went on, 'Let's throw this coin, and the winner can take the horse. Then nobody will feel bad. Yes?'

'OK,' the young Welsh soldier said. 'Heads!' he called, and the German threw the coin into the air. Both men looked when it fell to the ground.

'It's heads, so you win,' the older man said. 'Look after the horse.' He gave the rope to the British soldier. 'Now the fighting will start again. But we showed them, didn't we? We found a way to agree.'

The Welsh man smiled. 'I'd like to stay out here with you for a few hours and talk about this war,' he said. 'We could find a way to stop all of this. We could even throw a coin and see who wins.'

The German soldier laughed and put his hand on the young man's arm. 'Be careful, my friend,' he said, 'and good luck to you.'

'The same to you,' the young Welsh soldier replied. Then they turned around and walked back to their different trenches. The men on the British side were shouting and whistling while I limped towards them through the mud. They put me into a veterinary **wagon**, and two big, black horses pulled it along the road and away from the front line. The wagon was moving from side to side, and I soon fell. My leg was hurting badly and I couldn't stand up again, so I lay on the floor and closed my eyes.

When the wagon stopped, we were in a long yard with stables on both sides. Horses were looking over their stable doors and watching us. Orderlies helped me to stand up and get down from the wagon, and soon there were soldiers all around me. They patted me and talked.

'What are you all doing?' a sergeant shouted across the yard. 'Perhaps it's famous because they found it in no-man's-land, but it's only a horse. We've got three hundred horses in this hospital, so stop standing around and go back to work.'

Then the sergeant spoke to a young man behind me. 'And you. The major is coming to see this horse later, so wash and brush him. Right now, he's the dirtiest horse in the British army!'

'Yes, Sergeant Thunder!' the young man said.

'I know that voice,' I thought, 'but how?'

wagon a big car with sides and a top that horses pull

45

ACTIVITIES

READING CHECK

Correct the mistakes in these false sentences.

a Friedrich ~~sleeps~~ next to Topthorn's dead body. ......*dies*......

b The next morning Joey sees some soldiers and runs. ....

c He hurts his neck on some barbed wire. ....

d Joey can't see anything because of the rain. ....

e Two brave orderlies meet in no-man's-land. ....

f The Welsh man gives Joey some bread. ....

g The German throws a rope. ....

h The German soldier takes Joey back to his side. ....

i A wagon takes Joey to a farm. ....

j A sergeant tells a young soldier to look for Joey. ....

k Joey knows the young soldier's face. ....

WORD WORK

1 Match the words in the box with the pictures below and on page 47.

coin   handkerchief   ~~machine~~   mist
rope   sergeant   wagon

a ...*machine*...........   **b** ....   **c** ....

46

d ....

e ....

f ....

g ....

GUESS WHAT

What happens in the last chapter? Write *Yes*, *No* or *Perhaps*.

a Joey meets Albert again. ....

b Shells hit the stables and there is a fire. ....

c Albert's friend dies. ....

d Joey pulls a wagon again. ....

e The war finishes. ....

f The army wants to sell Joey. ....

g Joey sees Emilie again. ....

h Albert and Joey go back to England. ....

i Albert marries a girl from his village. ....

Chapter 8
Old friends

The young man took my rope and walked in front of me. I could just see the back of his head.

'There's mud all over you,' he said, 'but I'll wash you before the major comes. Then he can look at your leg.'

He started to whistle, and I knew who it was. It was Albert's voice and Albert's whistle! I neighed at him.

'It's OK,' he said. 'I won't hurt you.' There was mud and blood on me, and he couldn't see who I was.

'Are you talking to horses again?' a voice said. 'Why do you think that they understand you?' A young soldier came out of the nearest stable.

'Perhaps some horses don't,' Albert answered. 'But my Joey did. He was different, David. You'll know that when you see him.'

'There are half a million horses out there,' David said, 'and you came to France to look for *your* horse. How do you think that you're going to find him?'

'No horse is like Joey,' Albert replied. 'He's red-brown with a white star on his head and four white socks. I could find him in a thousand horses.'

'You're mad, Albert. You know that,' David laughed. 'But I'll help you to wash and brush this horse. You'll never finish it before the major gets here.' Albert worked on my back, and David washed my legs, head, and face. Slowly, I lost my coat of mud.

'Hey, Albert,' David said. 'This horse is red-brown. Did you say that Joey had white socks and a white star?'

'That's right,' Albert answered. 'Why?'

'Because under all this mud I can see a white star on this horse's head,' David cried excitedly, 'and four white socks!'

'Ha, ha – very funny!' said Albert. He sounded angry, but he stopped working and walked around me. Then suddenly his face changed.

He looked into my eyes. 'Joey?' he said. Then he turned to David. 'You're right. Perhaps this *is* Joey. There's one way to be sure.' He took the rope off me and walked away. Then he whistled. I limped towards him and put my head on his arm.

'It's really him, David!' Albert cried 'It's my Joey!'

For the next few days, I was truly happy. Albert was with me, and I had lots of sweet hay. I was famous at the hospital, and all the men visited me – even Sergeant Thunder.

'You're a fine horse,' the sergeant said, while he patted my head. 'So **get better**, do you hear?'

At first I began to feel stronger. But when I woke up one morning, my body hurt very badly. I couldn't eat my food, and it was difficult to move my legs.

'I'm sorry,' the major told Albert after he saw me. 'I know that you love this horse, but he's ill and he's going to die.'

'No!' cried Albert. 'We can save him, I know!'

get better to become well again after you are ill

49

'He's got **tetanus** from that barbed wire,' the major explained. 'Nearly every horse with tetanus dies. We should shoot him now before it really begins to hurt him.'

'But sir,' David said. 'You told us to fight for every horse's life. We can save him. All the men will help, sir.'

'Don't speak like that to the major!' Sergeant Thunder said. 'If there's any way to save Joey, I'm sure that Major Martin will try.'

The major looked quickly at the sergeant, then he said, 'All right, you can try to save him. Put a man in this stable twenty-four hours a day. The horse won't want to eat or drink, but if he doesn't, he'll die.'

They put a **harness** on me because I couldn't stand. I couldn't eat hay, so they gave me hot oats and milk. My body hurt more every day, but Albert and David never left me. They slept in the stable, and Albert talked to me late into the night.

tetanus you get this illness from dirty metal, and it can kill you

harness a number of belts that together hold an animal

One night, after weeks in the harness, I found that I could move my neck. I quietly neighed, and Albert and David woke up. Soon the stables were full of excited soldiers.

After that, I slowly began to feel better. A few weeks later, I was pulling a hay cart around the hospital. Then they put me to work pulling the veterinary wagon. With another horse and Albert, we brought wounded animals from the front line.

While we were walking towards the guns one morning, Albert told me about his girl. 'Maisie's her name, Joey,' he said. 'She's got beautiful blue eyes and she makes the best bread in the village. She doesn't understand horses, but she'll like you.'

When Albert brought my hay one evening, he sat down heavily in the stable. 'A shell hit David's wagon today,' he said. 'David was like a brother to me, Joey. He was just twenty years old, and now he's dead.' A few weeks later, the war ended. But Albert couldn't feel happy. Not after David's death.

Now the British army was going home. We waited for weeks as long lines of men, guns, and trucks went past the hospital. Then one day, Major Martin talked to the men.

'We're leaving later this week,' he said. 'But we can't take the horses. The army wants to sell them.'

There were angry voices around the yard. 'Sir, they're ill,' said Sergeant Thunder. 'And most of them will go to the **butchers**. You know that, don't you, sir?'

'I do, Sergeant,' the major replied, 'And I don't like it any more than you. But this is an army. We do what people tell us to do. We'll have the **auction** tomorrow morning.'

That night, the soldiers talked outside the stables. They were giving money to Sergeant Thunder. I heard Albert's voice.

'Is that all the money that we need for him?' he asked.

'I don't know,' the sergeant replied. 'But the major's given us all the money that he was saving, too. Let's hope so.'

The next day, the soldiers took us out into the yard one after the other. I was the last horse. There was a crowd in the yard, and Albert walked me around in circles. People were shouting,

butcher a man who sells meat

auction when you sell things to different people who give the most money for them

and a man at the front was calling **prices**. The sergeant was trying to buy me, and all of the orderlies were watching him, but the price went higher and higher.

'Twenty-five pounds from the sergeant,' shouted the man at the front. 'Twenty-six over there. Twenty-seven to the butcher from Cambrai! Any more than twenty-seven?'

The sergeant shook his head. He had just twenty-six pounds. The butcher from Cambrai smiled happily.

'Twenty-eight pounds!' shouted a voice from the back of the crowd. Everyone turned around. It was Emilie's grandfather, and he bought me at that price. After the auction, the old man talked to the sergeant. Then he walked towards us.

'You and I are both farmers, young man,' he said, while he shook Albert's hand, 'and I know that we both love this horse. So I'm going to sell him to you.'

Albert looked at him. 'But I don't have the money to buy him back from you,' he said.

'I know that,' the old man replied. 'So I'm selling him to you for one **penny** and a promise.'

Albert didn't understand.

'I've looked for this horse for a long time,' the old farmer explained. 'You see, we are old friends. Joey and another horse lived on my farm for about a year. We looked after them, and my granddaughter Emilie loved them.' He stopped speaking, and tears ran down his face.

'When the Germans took the horses from us,' he went on, 'Emilie became very ill. Before she died, I promised to find these horses and to give them a good home. I couldn't find the black horse, but in the end I found this one. So take your horse to England, but promise me something. Tell everyone there about my Emilie, and how she loved him.'

price the money that you must pay to buy something

penny a very small coin

Albert gave a penny to the old man and thanked him. After that, the old farmer kissed my nose lightly. 'Goodbye, my friend,' he said. Then he turned around and walked away.

A few days later, we were back in England. Albert rode me proudly into his home village in Devon. They called us **heroes** there, but the real heroes of the war never came home. They were lying out there in the fields of France with Captain Nicholls, Emilie, Topthorn, Friedrich, and David.

And so I worked on the farm again with my dear old friend Zoey. Even Albert's father was kind to me now. I think that he was sorry because Albert went to France for me. My dear Albert married his girl, Maisie, and he was right about her – she made very nice bread. Maisie and I never became real friends, but we learnt to live together because Albert loved us both.

hero a person who does something brave or good

READING CHECK

Match the characters with events from the story.

Joey

Albert

David

Sergeant Thunder

Major Martin

Emilie's grandfather

Albert's father

Maisie

a ....Maisie........................... marries Albert.

b .... says that Joey will die.

c .... has mud all over him when he arrives at the hospital.

d .... asks Albert to promise something.

e .... dies in the last days of the war.

f .... talks to Joey at night when he is ill.

g .... can't buy Joey at the auction.

h .... feels sorry for what he did, and is nice to Joey.

ACTIVITIES

WORD WORK

1 Unscramble the words from Chapter 8 in the coins.

a **teg ttereb** …get better… b **nepny** …………………

c **chertub** ………………… d **ehro** …………………

e **antetus** ………………… f **actnoiu** …………………

g **iprce** ………………… h **neharss** …………………

2 Use the correct form of the words from Activity 1 to complete the summary of Chapter 8.

For a few days Albert and Joey were happy. But then Joey became very ill with
a) …tetanus… . They put him in a **b)** ………………… because he couldn't stand, and
Albert and David looked after him day and night. Slowly, he began to **c)** ………………… .

Albert's friend David died in the last days of the war. When the war ended, the army
wanted to sell all the horses. Sergeant Thunder tried to buy Joey for Albert at the
d) …………………, but the **e)** ………………… was too high. A **f)** ………………… wanted to
buy Joey for horse meat, but at the last minute, Emilie's grandfather bought him. The old man
wanted Joey to have a good home, so he sold him to Albert for one **g)** ………………… .

A few days later, Albert rode Joey into their village in England. People called them
h) …………………, but they didn't feel brave or special. They just remembered their
dead friends.

GUESS WHAT

What happens after the story ends? Answer the questions.

a How does Joey feel about Albert's father now that he's back on the farm?
b A lot of characters die in the story. Which of them does Joey miss the most?
c Why is the painting of Joey in the village and not at the farm?
d What do you think happens to …
 ● Trooper Warren and Captain Stewart?
 ● Emilie's grandfather?
 ● Sally, the girl from Trooper Warren's village?

Project A *Different points of view*

1 **Read the description of how Albert trains Joey to plough on page 8. Who tells the story?**

2 **Match the descriptions of the same events with these people. Use some people more than once.**

I nearly shot that horse after he kicked me, but I had a bet with Farmer Easton. I couldn't win a bet with a dead horse, could I?

a ...Albert's father.....

I was cooking dinner when my husband came in. He was limping. 'I'm going to kill that animal,' he shouted.

b ....

Joey smelt of sweat, and I knew that he was very tired, but I had to use the whip when he tried to stop. I felt terrible, but it was the only way to train him.

c ....

When Albert ploughed the field, I was watching from Mr Narracott's house. The horses ploughed well, I have to say.

d ....

Joey couldn't pull the plough in a straight line at first, but Zoey showed him what to do. She saved us both, I think.

e ....

I always do what I promise. So after I won the bet, I told Albert that Joey could stay.

f ....

I was very surprised when I lost the bet. I didn't think that they could teach that stupid horse to do anything.

g ....

Albert

Farmer Easton

Albert's mother

Albert's father

3 Use the words in the boxes to complete two 'point of view' descriptions of the cavalry charge on page 20.

blood   fell   wounded   enemy   charged   ground   ~~swords~~   machine guns

The officers shouted, and we took out our **a)** ...*swords*... . When we **b)** ....

out of the wood, I heard the sound of **c)** .... Suddenly, my horse

d) ...., and I was on the **e)** .... I could taste **f)** .... in

my mouth, but I knew that I wasn't **g)** .... I lay next to my dead horse while my

unit galloped towards the **h)** .... Then I stood up and ran after them.

(*Trooper Warren's point of view*)

hot   prisoners   smell   reached   cavalry   ammunition   grass

We were walking through the long **i)** .... in a field. It was a **j)** ....,

sunny afternoon, and I could **k)** .... some red flowers at my feet. Suddenly,

we heard a shout. British **l)** .... were charging down the hill towards us! It all

happened very quickly. When the first horses **m)** .... us, my friend Dieter was

shooting at them with our machine gun, and I was trying to open an **n)** .... box.

A few minutes later, we were **o)** ....

(*A German soldier's point of view*)

4 Choose one of the events below and write a description of it from another character's point of view. Think about these things.

- Who and where are you?
- What is happening?
- What can you see and hear?
- Can you touch, taste or smell anything?
- How do you feel?

(See page 26)

(See pages 43– 45)

Project B *War art*

1 Choose the best words to complete the description of the painting.

Over the Top by John Nash

The painting **a)** *looks at* / *shows* a battle in the First World War. In the **b)** *foreground* /
background, a British soldier is climbing out of a trench. Behind him, **c)** *at the bottom* / *in the
middle* of the picture, more soldiers are walking into no-man's-land. You can **d)** *tell* / *know*
that the Germans are shooting at them because **e)** *there* / *those* are dead men in the trench
on the **f)** *right* / *left* of the painting, and also in the snow. It isn't night, but the sky is dark and
we can see clouds of smoke at the **g)** *top right* / *bottom left* of the picture. A shell has just hit
the ground in the **h)** *background* / *foreground*, throwing snow and men into the air.

PROJECTS

2 Use the words in the box to complete the description of the painting.

behind	front
battle	rider
across	another
cavalry	officer

The Charge at Moreuil Wood
by Sir Alfred Munnings

This painting shows a British **a)** .... charge in World War I. It's early in the morning, and the troopers are holding their swords and charging **b)** .... a field. There is a line of horses in the foreground, and **c)** .... line **d)** .... them in the background. At the top of the painting, we can see a wood. At the bottom left of the picture, an **e)** .... on a black horse is riding in **f)** .... of his men, shouting to them. At the bottom right of the painting, a horse is falling and another horse has lost its **g)** .... , so we know that they are in a **h)** .... and not just training.

3 Write notes to answer these questions about the painting in Activity 2.

a What does the picture show?
b What time of day is it?
c What can you see in the foreground?
d What can you see in the background?
e What other interesting details can you see, and where are they?
(e.g. in the bottom left and right of this painting)

Menin Road by Paul Nash

After the Recapture of Bapaume
by Christopher Nevinson

4 Choose one of the paintings above and write notes to answer the questions.

What does the picture show?

....

What time of day or time of year do you think it is?

....

What can you see in the foreground?

....

What can you see in the background?

....

What other interesting details can you see, and where are they?

....

5 Use your notes to write a description of the painting that you chose in Activity 4.

6 Make a copy of your painting. Use the picture and your description to make a war art poster for your classroom wall.

GRAMMAR

GRAMMAR CHECK

so, *but* and *because*

We use so to talk about a result of something that happens.

Zoey was with us, so I didn't feel worried.

We use because to talk about a reason why something happens.

She usually rode me because Topthorn was taller.

We use but to contrast two pieces of information.

Maisie and I never became friends, but we learnt to live together.

1 Complete the sentences with *so*, *but* or *because* and the information in the box.

his father had a bet with Farmer Easton	Albert's father won the bet
Zoey showed him what to do	Albert's mother stopped him
Joey never forgot what he did at the animal market	he didn't like Farmer Easton
the horse kicked him	he tried to stay away from him

a Albert's father wasn't a bad man, *but Joey never forgot what he did at the animal market.*

b Joey was afraid of Albert's father …

....

c One night, Albert's father was angry with Joey …

....

d He went to get his gun, …

....

e Albert had to teach Joey to plough …

....

f It wasn't easy for Joey to pull the plough, …

....

g The horses ploughed well, …

....

h Albert's father was happy …

....

61

GRAMMAR CHECK

Indefinite pronouns and adverbs

We use indefinite pronouns ending in -body/one and -thing instead of nouns to talk about people and things in a general way.

We can't see anything in the mist.

We use singular verb forms with indefinite pronouns.

Nobody wants to go to war.

We use indefinite adverbs ending in -where instead of a preposition.

There were dead horses and men everywhere.

The table shows when to use which indefinite pronoun.

People	Things	Places
everyone / everybody	*everything*	*everywhere*
no one / nobody	*nothing*	*nowhere*
someone / somebody (+)	*something* (+)	*somewhere* (+)
anyone / anybody (– / ?)	*anything* (– / ?)	*anywhere* (– / ?)

2 Rewrite the sentences. Replace the underlined words with indefinite pronouns and adverbs.

a We couldn't find the enemy <u>in any place</u>.

....We couldn't find the enemy anywhere....

b We often stopped, and the soldiers gave us <u>a little food</u> to eat.

....

c One day, <u>a trooper</u> saw the enemy on the other side of a wood.

....

d <u>All the men</u> felt excited before the battle.

....

e We charged, and then <u>all the things</u> happened very fast.

....

f Suddenly there was <u>no rider</u> on my back. I couldn't do <u>a thing</u>, so I ran on towards the enemy.

....

g There were dead horses <u>all around</u>. I wanted to run away, but there was <u>no place</u> to go.

....

GRAMMAR CHECK

could and *couldn't*

We use could and couldn't to talk about ability in the past.

Nobody could be happy for long in that war.

My leg was hurting badly, and I couldn't stand up.

3 Complete the sentences with *could* or *couldn't*.

a Albert didn't want his father to sell Joey, but he ...couldn't... stop him.

b He .... go to war with Joey because he was too young.

c Captain Nicholls .... draw horses very well.

d Joey tried to throw Perkins off his back, but he .... do it.

e Joey and Topthorn .... gallop faster than the other horses in their unit.

f Trooper Warren didn't want to go to war, but he .... say 'no'.

g The army .... use cavalry in the winter because the ground was too soft for cavalry horses.

h The troopers didn't have to fight. They .... rest during the winter.

i We were still near the front line, and we .... hear the guns.

4 Complete Trooper Warren's description of the cavalry charge with *could* or *couldn't* and the words in the box.

| cross   fight   find   go   hear   jump   ~~see~~   see   stop |

We **a)** ...could see... a wood in front of us, and long lines of barbed wire. We started to gallop. We **b)** .... anything at first, but then the shells started to fall loudly. Horses and men fell all around us, but we **c)** .... to help them. The machine guns were killing more and more of us. Most of us never reached the barbed wire, and very few of us **d)** .... a way through it, but I was lucky. I **e)** .... Captain Stewart in front of me. He found a place where he **f)** .... the barbed wire and went into the wood. I followed him because I knew that Joey **g)** .... over the wire. Suddenly, German soldiers came out from behind the trees. We **h)** .... back because they were all around us. We were alone in the wood, and we **i)** .... the Germans so we dropped our swords.

GRAMMAR CHECK

Question tags

We use question tags when we want to check information that we are not sure of or when we want to ask someone to agree with us.

When the sentence is affirmative, the tag is negative. *My father sold Joey to you, didn't he?*

When the sentence is negative, the tag is positive. *I can't do anything, can I?*

5 **Match the first and second parts of these questions.**

a These animals were British cavalry horses,
b Their riders didn't die in the battle,
c The horses pull the hospital wagon now,
d The orderlies don't know how to look after them,
e They're staying on a French farm,
f The farmer will look after them,
g He's got stables to put the horses in,
h They won't go to the front line again today,
i They've saved a lot of lives,

1 haven't they?
2 do they?
3 won't he?
4 hasn't he?
5 weren't they?
6 will they?
7 don't they?
8 did they?
9 aren't they?

6 **Write the question tags to complete the conversation between Albert and Sergeant Thunder.**

Thunder: You love this horse, **a)** .don't you.?

Albert: Yes, I do. But he's very ill, **b)** ....?

Thunder: Yes, he is. You heard the major. But we can save him, **c)** ....?

Albert: Tetanus hurts a lot, **d)** ....?

Thunder: Yes, it does. His head and neck will hurt and he won't want to eat. But he's a fighter, **e)** ....?

Albert: Yes. He won't die, **f)** ...., Sergeant?

Thunder: No, I think he'll live. And I'm never wrong, **g)** ....?

Albert: No, Sergeant. He didn't come out of no-man's-land to die in a stable, **h)** ....?

Thunder: No, son. Now get the harness. We haven't got all day, **i)** ....?

GRAMMAR CHECK

Reported commands and requests

We use told + (not) to + the infinitive to report commands.

'Move!' → *Friedrich told Joey to move.*

We use ask + (not) to + the infinitive to report requests.

'Please come back.' → *Emilie asked the horses to come back.*

Note that pronouns and possessive adjectives may change.

'Don't shoot us.' → *They told the soldiers not to shoot them.*

'Drop your sword, Trooper.' → *Captain Stewart told Trooper Warren to drop his sword.*

7 Rewrite these incorrect sentences.

a Albert's mother told him not talk to horses.

......*Albert's mother told him not to talk to horses.*...............

b Albert told Joey not kick to anyone again.

....

c Albert asked his father don't hit Joey.

....

d The vet told to Captain Nicholls buy the horse.

....

e Albert asked the captain take him to the war with Joey.

....

8 Report the speakers' words. Complete the sentences.

a 'Do your best,' Trooper Warren told Joey.

Trooper Warren told Joey ...*to do his best*...............

b 'Please don't give them my horses.'

Emilie asked her grandfather ....

c 'Please think of Emilie.'

Emilie's grandfather asked the horses ....

d 'Come with me.'

Friedrich told Joey ....

e 'Have your guns ready.'

The sergeant told his men ....

GRAMMAR CHECK

Participle phrases

In stories, we often talk about two actions that happen at the same time.

'Get in there, Zoey!' the man shouted. He hit her.

If the subject is the same for both verbs, it often sounds better to combine the sentences. We add a comma after the first verb phrase, then use the -ing form of the second verb.

'Get in there, Zoey!' the man shouted, hitting her.

9 Use participle phrases to combine the pairs of sentences.

a Emilie lay in her room. She was fighting for her life.
 Emilie lay in her room, fighting for her life.

b The doctor stayed with her. He did everything that he could.
 ....

c On Christmas morning, we walked to the front line. We thought of Emilie.
 ....

d Heavy snow was falling. It hid the holes in the road.
 ....

e A shell hit the road behind us. It shook the ground.
 ....

f Wounded men sat on the cart. They sang Christmas songs.
 ....

g We went to and from the front line all day. We saved a lot of lives.
 ....

h We got back to the farm at night. We were feeling very tired.
 ....

GRAMMAR CHECK

Conditional sentences

We use if + present simple + will future to talk about the results of a possible situation.

If you don't come back, I'll die.

We use if + present simple + imperative to tell or ask someone to do something in a possible situation.

If you want to live, come with me.

The if clause can come at the start or the end of the sentence. When it comes at the start, we put a comma after it.

If you understand me, think of Emilie. Think of Emilie if you understand me.

0 Match the first and second parts of the sentences. Then write the speakers.

> Emilie   Sergeant Thunder   Captain Nicholls   Friedrich
> ~~Albert's father~~   Major Martin   Emilie's grandfather

a If you give me any trouble,

b Bring the horse tomorrow

c I'll always look after you

d If you can understand me

e Come with me

f If there's a way to save Joey,

g If this horse doesn't eat,

1 Major Martin will try. ....

2 if you stay here with me. ....

3 if you want to live! ....

4 I'll hit you. ..Albert's father......

5 he will die. ....

6 if you want to sell him. ....

7 please think of Emilie tonight. ....

1 Use the words in the box in the correct form to complete the sentences.

> be   come   marry   not learn   ~~not shoot~~   take   want

a 'If you love Albert, ..don't shoot.....his horse.'

b 'If you ....to keep Joey, teach him to pull a plough.'

c 'Joey ....anything if you hit him.'

d 'If we're still at war when you're seventeen, ...and find me.'

e 'If I live through this war, I ....Sally.'

f 'If we don't give the horses to the German major, he ....them from us.'

g 'If the price ....too high, we won't have the money to buy your horse.'

DOMINOES
THE STRUCTURED APPROACH TO READING IN ENGLISH

Dominoes is an enjoyable series of illustrated classic and modern stories in four carefully graded language stages – from Starter to Three – which take learners from beginner to intermediate level.

Each *Domino* reader includes:
- a good story to read and enjoy
- integrated activities to develop reading skills and increase active vocabulary
- personalized projects to make the language and story themes more meaningful
- seven pages of grammar activities for consolidation.

Each *Domino* pack contains a reader, plus a MultiROM with:
- a complete audio recording of the story, fully dramatized to bring it to life
- interactive activities to offer further practice in reading and language skills and to consolidate learning.

If you liked this Level Two *Domino*, why not read these?

V is for Vampire
Lesley Thompson

`He's great, Vera,' said Angie.

When Viktor Sarav takes a job at Ballantine's, Angie and her brother Don – the young owners of the New York fashion company – are pleased. But soon there are strange deaths in the company. Is there a vampire at work at Ballantine's? Vera Donato, a company director with secrets to hide, is against Viktor. But Ed Valdemar, the company lawyer, trusts him. Who is right?

Book ISBN: 978 0 19 424983 6
MultiROM Pack ISBN: 978 0 19 424967 6

The Curse of Capistrano
Johnston McCulley

'Señor Zorro is on the road again, they say,' the landlord began.
'Why do I always hear his name?' cried Sergeant Gonzales angrily.

Zorro fights to help the poor and weak in California under the Spanish Governor's rule. Sergeant Gonzales has promised to catch and kill him, so how does Zorro always escape? And how will Señorita Lolita – the only daughter of a fine but poor old family – choose between Zorro, the exciting outlaw, and Don Diego, the rich but boring young man who wants to marry her?

Book ISBN: 978 0 19 424924 9
MultiROM Pack ISBN: 978 0 19 424923 2

You can find details and a full list of books in the Oxford Graded Readers catalogue and Oxford English Language Teaching Catalogue, and on the website: www.oup.com/elt

Teachers: see www.oup.com/elt for a full range of online support, or consult your local office.

	CEFR	Cambridge Exams	IELTS	TOEFL iBT	TOEIC
Level 3	B1	PET	4.0	57-86	550
Level 2	A2–B1	KET-PET	3.0-4.0	–	–
Level 1	A1–A2	YLE Flyers/KET	3.0	–	–
Starter & Quick Starter	A1	YLE Movers	–	–	–